PREVIEW

Rancher Mac Brazel scanned the horizon. He was in the desert outside Roswell, New Mexico, looking for lost sheep. Out of the corner of his eye, he noticed something shiny.

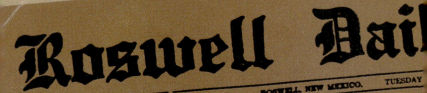

## The Wreckage

There were odd bits of metal foil strewn across the ground. Brazel got closer and saw strips of rubber, too, as well as pieces of tape with strange designs.

Something seemed to have crashed in the desert. But what?

## Flying Objects

Weeks later, Brazel gathered up some of the debris. Then he headed for Roswell. When he arrived, he got another surprise. People were claiming to have seen unidentified flying objects, or UFOs.

## *The Mystery*

Had Brazel found the wreckage of a UFO? He handed over the debris to a U.S. military air base. Astonishingly, a colonel said the debris was the remains of a "flying disc" from outer space! But other military officials in Texas quickly denied the story.

## *The Question*

How would investigators uncover the real story behind the wreckage? And what would it take to prove or disprove the existence of UFOs?

## PREVIEW PHOTOS

**PAGES 2-3:** On July 8, 1947, the *Roswell Daily Record* reported that a flying saucer had been found on a ranch near Roswell.
**PAGES 4-5:** A military official examines the debris that Mac Brazel had given to authorities.

**Book Design:** Red Herring Design/NYC **Photo Credits:** Photographs © 2012: age fotostock/Walter Bibikow: 26, 27; Alamy Images: 21 top left (ImageState), 8 (Luc Novovitch); AP Images/Air Force: 33; Corbis Images/Bettmann: 18; Dreamstime.com/Frenta: back cover foreground; Everett Collection, Inc.: 44 bottom (Columbia Pictures), 45 center left (Orion Pictures), 45 center right (Paramount), 45 bottom right (Universal), 45 top left (Warner Brothers), 44 top; Fortean Picture Library: 2, 3, 4, 5, 16, 30; Getty Images: 1 (Matthias Clamer), 38 (Joshua Roberts), 22 (Chip Simons), 20 (United States Air Force); iStockphoto/Clint Spencer: 10; NASA/Greatest Images of NASA ; 42, 43; NEWSCOM: 29 bottom (Daily Mirror), 36 (Timothy J. Jones/iPhoto.ca), 14 (Zhang Luqiao/ChinaFotoPress), 29 center (Mike Nelson/AFP), 34 center (Splash News); Photo Researchers, NY: 34 bottom (Julian Baum), 40 (Dr. Seth Shostak); Photofest: 45 top right (Cinecom Pictures), 44 center (Columbia Pictures), 45 top center (United Artists); ShutterStock, Inc.: 29 top (DGDesign), 28 (Brian Guest), 21 bottom right (Mike Heywood), 41 (Caitlin Mirra), back cover background, cover, 35 (photoBeard); The Granger Collection, New York: 34 top; The Image Works: 24 (Michael Buhler/Mary Evans Picture Library), 25 (Fortean), 15 left, 21 bottom left ( Mary Evans Picture Library), 15 right, 21 top right, 39 (Topham), 12 (UPP).

With thanks to N. B. Grace

Library of Congress Cataloging-in-Publication Data
Peterkin, P. A.
UFO lands in USA! : was spacecraft crash covered up? / P. A. Peterkin.
p. cm. — (XBOOKS)
Includes bibliographical references and index.
ISBN-13: 978-0-545-32947-7
ISBN-10: 0-545-32947-7
1. Unidentified flying objects—Sightings and encounters—New Mexico—Roswell—Juvenile literature. I. Peterkin, P. A. UFOs. II. Title.
TL789.5.N6P47 2012
001.942—dc22     2011010425

No part of this publication may be reproduced in whole or in part, or stored in a retrieval system, or transmitted in any form or by any means, electronic, mechanical, photocopying, recording, or otherwise, without written permission of the publisher. For information regarding permission, write to Scholastic Inc., 557 Broadway, New York, NY 10012.

Copyright © 2012, 2008 by Scholastic Inc.

All rights reserved. Published by Scholastic Inc. Printed in the U.S.A.

SCHOLASTIC, XBOOKS, and associated logos are trademarks and/or registered trademarks of Scholastic Inc.

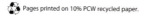 Pages printed on 10% PCW recycled paper.

1 2 3 4 5 6 7 8 9 10     40    21 20 19 18 17 16 15 14 13 12

# *UFO Lands in USA!*

## Was Spacecraft Crash Covered Up?

P. A. PETERKIN

**THIS ALIEN DUMMY** is on display at the International UFO Museum and Research Center in Roswell, New Mexico.

# TABLE OF CONTENTS

**PREVIEW** ............... 1

### CHAPTER 1
## Wreckage in Roswell ........... 10
Did a flying saucer crash in the desert?

**Where's the Proof?** ..... 14

### CHAPTER 2
## It Fell From the Sky ..................... 16
First one story, then another. Is somebody lying?

**Close Encounters** ....... 21

### CHAPTER 3
## The Truth Is Out There ...... 22
Is the U.S. military hiding alien bodies?

**Project Blue Book** ...... 28

### CHAPTER 4
## Mystery Solved? ........ 30
A top-secret project goes public . . . finally!

**Visitors Welcome!** ...... 34

### CHAPTER 5
## The Debate Continues ..... 36
Spy balloons? Crash-test dummies? Some people just don't believe it.

**XFILES** ................. 39

**Are We Alone?** ......... 40

**This Is for All You Lonely Aliens** ........... 42

**And ... *ACTION!*** ......... 44

# 1

# *Wreckage in Roswell*

## Did a flying saucer crash in the desert?

On the night of June 13, 1947, a fierce storm battered the lonely desert around Roswell, New Mexico. The next morning, rancher W. W. "Mac" Brazel saddled up his horse and rode out to look for sheep that had been scattered by the storm.

On his rounds, Brazel came across a field full of strange wreckage. Wandering through the mess, he found odd-looking rubber strips, metal foil, and sheets of very tough paper. Some of the debris had pieces of tape covered with strange flowerlike designs.

Brazel was in a hurry at the time. He had to find his sheep. But three weeks later he returned to the field. He filled bags with some of the debris and set off for Roswell.

When he got there, the town was buzzing. People were talking about strange newspaper reports.

**SILVER FOIL was among the debris found by rancher Mac Brazel. It's displayed here on a plate printed with a newspaper article about the event.**

## *Strange Aircraft*

According to one newspaper story, on June 24 a pilot in Washington State reported seeing nine strange aircraft zoom past his plane at 1,200 miles per hour. (That's pretty fast! The average speed of a modern passenger jet is about 575 miles per hour.)

Dozens of other people came forward with similar tales. Each of them claimed to have seen unidentified flying objects, or UFOs. Reporters started calling the UFOs "flying saucers" or "flying discs."

Was it possible that Brazel had found the remains of a flying saucer? The rancher went straight to the town sheriff with his story. The sheriff decided to contact military officials at the nearby Roswell Army Air Field. It was home to bomber aircraft armed with nuclear weapons.

On July 7, Brazel and the sheriff called the base. The story they told launched the most enduring UFO mystery of all time.

## IN DEPTH

# Where's the Proof?

### Scientists insist on evidence to confirm that UFOs come from outer space.

When it comes to UFOs, people tend to be either believers or skeptics.

The believers think that UFO sightings prove that aliens have come to Earth. The skeptics doubt that aliens have visited Earth. They want evidence to prove that people who say they've seen alien spacecraft aren't lying or mistaken.

What would it take for someone to prove the existence of UFOs from outer space? Scientists require data, or evidence, to confirm that a claim is true.

Here are a few types of evidence that UFO believers have offered as proof that aliens have come to Earth. Does any of this seem like reliable evidence to you?

## Eyewitness accounts.
**EVIDENCE?** Many people claim they have seen UFOs or aliens. These eyewitnesses are often described as level-headed. (Former U.S. president Jimmy Carter said he saw a UFO.)
**OR NOT?** Even trustworthy witnesses can be confused.

**THIS PHOTO OF A UFO** was taken in Japan in 1957.

## Photographic proof.
**EVIDENCE?** Some eyewitnesses have taken photographs of what they claim are UFOs. And some of the pictures look remarkably real.
**OR NOT?** It's pretty easy to fake a photo.

## Physical evidence.
**EVIDENCE?** Broken branches and packed-down soil have been found at places where UFOs are said to have landed. Isn't that proof that a spaceship landed at that spot?
**OR NOT?** There could be plenty of other explanations, too.

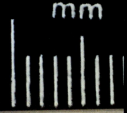

**THIS OBJECT** was removed from the roof of someone's mouth. The person claimed it had been implanted by aliens.

## Personal experience.
**EVIDENCE?** Many people claim to have been abducted by aliens. Some even say aliens implanted objects inside them.
**OR NOT?** Strange items have been removed from peoples' bodies. But there's no proof that these objects came from beyond Earth.

## No other explanation.
**EVIDENCE?** Some UFO sightings just can't be explained. So doesn't that prove the existence of aliens?
**OR NOT?** Absolutely not, say the skeptics. "Unexplained cases are simply unexplained," writes scientist Hudson Hoagland. He says that a lack of explanation never counts as evidence.

**MAC BRAZEL** found the mysterious debris on this ranch near Roswell, New Mexico.

## 2

# It Fell From the Sky

### First one story, then another. Is somebody lying?

Major Jesse Marcel, an intelligence officer at Roswell Army Air Field, took up the case of the mysterious wreckage. Marcel and another officer met Mac Brazel at the field where he had found the debris. The men dug through the wreckage and tried to piece together an object they could recognize.

The officers gave up after a couple of hours. The debris was too unusual. Marcel collected the material

**U.S. ARMY OFFICERS** examine the debris found near Roswell. The military concluded that it was material from a crashed weather balloon.

and took it back to the air field. But no one at the base could identify it either.

A colonel at Roswell Army Air Field released a shocking statement. The army, he said, had discovered a "flying disc" from outer space. The next day, newspapers across the United States reported the astonishing story.

## A Simple Explanation

In the meantime, the wreckage had been sent to the Eighth Army Air Force headquarters in Texas. A general there quickly denied the colonel's report. The materials, the general said, had not come from outer space. They were simply the remains of a weather balloon. He invited reporters to his office to examine the debris.

The reporters left the meeting satisfied. The following day newspapers reported that the "flying disc" had been explained. The mystery of the UFO was solved. Or so it seemed. Most people accepted the explanation. They had no reason to doubt the army. But years later, Major Jesse Marcel, the intelligence officer from Roswell Army Air Field, spoke out.

## Strange Material

In 1978, just before he died, Marcel told a tabloid newspaper called the *National Enquirer* that the army had lied. The materials shown to reporters in 1947, he claimed, were not the materials he had picked up in the desert. The debris from the desert had strange qualities, he said. The metal foil couldn't be burned with a blowtorch or dented with a sledgehammer. It was, he said, "like nothing made on Earth."

**MAJOR JESSE MARCEL** shows the mysterious debris in 1947. In 1978, he claimed that this was not the debris he had seen at the crash site.

**IN DEPTH**

# *Close Encounters*

## What do you call a UFO sighting? It depends on how close you get.

People who study UFOs refer to UFO sightings as "close encounters." There are four types of close encounters:

### *Close Encounter of the First Kind*
Seeing a UFO from a distance

### *Close Encounter of the Third Kind*
Seeing an alien

### *Close Encounter of the Second Kind*
Seeing a UFO that leaves physical evidence behind (like the supposed alien remains below)

### *Close Encounter of the Fourth Kind*
Being abducted by aliens. Even many UFO researchers are skeptical about whether abductions have ever really occurred.

**YEARS AFTER** the Roswell incident, witnesses claimed they had seen the U.S. military remove bodies from the site. This alien dummy is based on their descriptions.

# 3

# *The Truth Is Out There*

## Is the U.S. military hiding alien bodies?

Major Jesse Marcel's story reopened the Roswell case. A flood of UFO researchers headed for New Mexico. The researchers found hundreds of people who claimed to know something about the crash. And many of these witnesses had strange stories to tell. They insisted that metal and rubber weren't the only things found in the desert in June 1947. Alien bodies had fallen to Earth as well.

A man named Grady L. Barnett said he had seen

**AN EYEWITNESS CLAIMED** that he had seen the U.S. military removing alien bodies from a crashed UFO.

debris from a flying saucer near Mac Brazel's ranch. Next to the wreckage lay four small bodies. The creatures had tiny arms and legs, big heads, and large slanted eyes. Barnett said the military took the bodies away. They told him not to talk about what he had seen.

Frank Kaufman had worked at the Roswell Army Air Field in 1947. He claimed that five alien bodies were recovered from the crash. According to Kaufman, the aliens had ash-colored skin, big eyes, fine features, and no hair. "They were very good-looking people," he said.

Witness after witness told stories of alien bodies

that had been taken away in secrecy. Had the U.S. military found evidence of life from outer space?

## Hangar 18

Many people who followed the Roswell mystery said yes. And they claimed that the army had a top-secret lab where they studied alien life-forms and UFOs. That lab was believed to be in Hangar 18 at the Wright-Patterson Air Force Base near Dayton, Ohio.

Several people told stories about Hangar 18. One former army pilot said that in 1953, he saw five crates delivered to Hangar 18. He said each crate contained

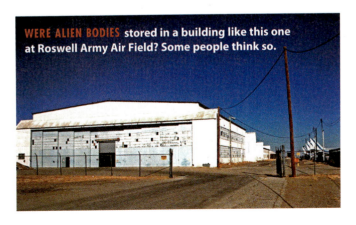

**WERE ALIEN BODIES** stored in a building like this one at Roswell Army Air Field? Some people think so.

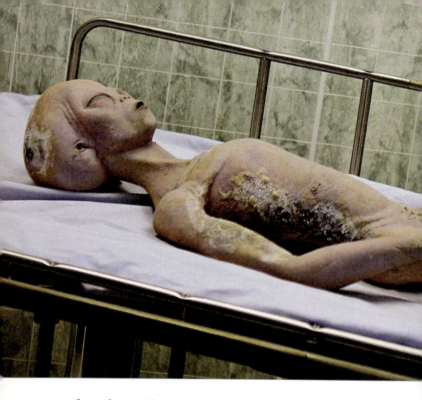

a four-foot-tall body with a large, bald head. The bodies were floating in a thick, blue liquid.

A military doctor claimed that in the 1950s he had performed an autopsy on an alien. (An autopsy is a surgical examination of a dead body.) His description sounded like countless others. The alien's head was "pear-shaped" and "oversized." It had no eyelids.

A lieutenant colonel at Wright-Patterson claimed that the Roswell debris was studied in Hangar 18.

**THIS EXHIBIT** at the International UFO Museum and Research Center shows an alien dummy on an autopsy table.

Most people at the base, he claimed, agreed that the debris had come from outer space.

And an army colonel named Philip J. Corso said that the debris was sent to his office in Washington, D.C., in the 1960s. He claimed that he turned it over to scientists in private industry. He told the scientists that the debris had come from foreign countries. According to Corso, the debris was used to create lasers and other amazing advances in technology.

# Project Blue Book

## Did the U.S. military secretly investigate UFOs? Yes. And no.

Yes, the U.S. military investigated UFO sightings. The investigation, called Project Blue Book, was carried out by the U.S. Air Force. But no, it was not a secret. Officers working on the project regularly reported their findings to the press.

Between 1952 and 1969, Project Blue Book looked into more than 12,000 UFO reports. Then, in 1969, the air force closed the office. It concluded that there was no evidence of alien contact.

According to Project Blue Book, the vast majority of these UFO reports fell into one of the following four categories.

### Conventional Objects

Many UFOs turned out to be planes, balloons, or even flocks of birds. The air force admitted that some were its own spy planes. Military officials had lied to keep them secret.

**IN DEPTH**

### *Atmospheric or Astronomical Events*
Some kinds of weather, such as ball lightning (left), look very unusual. Bright stars and strange-looking clouds have also been mistaken for UFOs.

### *First-Person Accounts*
Chuck Clark (shown at left) is an amateur astronomer. He's pointing toward an area in the desert where he believes the military studies aliens. But can he prove it? Not without evidence.

*Hoaxes* A small number of UFO sightings were deliberate pranks. This "flying saucer" (right) was part of an elaborate prank in the United Kingdom.

**IN 1994, THE AIR FORCE** claimed that the debris found near Roswell was the wreckage of a top-secret spy balloon like this one.

# 4

# Mystery Solved?

## A top-secret project goes public . . . finally!

The U.S. Air Force kept silent on the Roswell incident for nearly four decades. Then it finally came forward with its explanation of the mystery. In 1994, the air force released a report claiming that there had never been any aliens. And there certainly had never been any alien autopsies!

The report did include one surprising piece of news. In 1947, the U.S. Army had conducted a secret operation in New Mexico. It was called Project Mogul.

## *Top-Secret Balloons*

Project Mogul began in June 1947 when the U.S. Army launched four top-secret observation balloons. They were designed to detect nuclear-bomb tests 10,000 miles away in the Soviet Union. One of the balloons disappeared after high winds blew it off course.

According to the U.S. Air Force, the balloons were made of materials identical to the debris that Mac Brazel found. But the high-tech materials were so unusual that no one at the Roswell base knew what they were. The report even had an explanation for the flowered tape. It had been made at a toy factory.

But what about the alien bodies? The air force suggested two explanations. They might have been crash-test dummies dropped from high-altitude balloons (crash-test dummies are used to simulate what would happen to humans in an accident). Or they might have been the victims of a plane crash in which 11 people burned to death. These events didn't happen until the 1950s. But, as the air force pointed out, memories can get foggy after so many years.

**THE AIR FORCE CLAIMED** that the so-called aliens were actually crash-test dummies like these, dropped from spy balloons.

# Visitors Welcome!

**Were these sightings of real aliens—or could there be other explanations?**

| What happened, and when? | | Where? |
|---|---|---|
| **The Lubbock Lights** <br> August 31, 1951 |  | Lubbock, Texas |
| **A Real Alien Autopsy?** <br> August 28, 1995 | 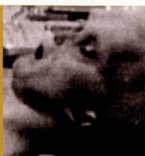 | American television |
| **A Flying Cigar?** <br> March 1987 |  | Belleville, Wisconsin |

# IN DEPTH

| What's the story? | UFO, or not? |
|---|---|
| A teenager took this picture of the Lubbock Lights. Between August and November, about 100 people saw lights in a crescent formation streaking across the sky. Among the first to observe the lights were three university professors. | Probably not, but no one has come up with a satisfying explanation. Military officials investigated. They decided that the UFOs were most likely migrating birds reflecting the city lights. |
| Millions of people watched a TV show called *Alien Autopsy: Fact or Fiction?* It featured clips from a film that supposedly had been shot in Roswell in 1947. It showed military doctors operating on what were said to be alien bodies. | No. In 2006 a special-effects expert named John Humphreys admitted that he created models of aliens for the film. |
| Between January and March, there were four UFO sightings in the town of Belleville. Some residents there saw cylinder-shaped objects like this one. They supposedly rose up out of forests—in broad daylight. | Possibly. Many eyewitnesses saw something strange. Illinois Air Traffic Control, which monitors flights in the airspace above Belleville, even reported a UFO in the area. But there's no proof that what people saw was from outer space. |

**A ROAD SIGN** marks the site of what some still claim was a UFO crash.

**5**

# *The Debate Continues*

## Spy balloons? Crash-test dummies? Some people just don't believe it.

The U.S. military had finally explained its role in the Roswell incident. But its report about high-tech balloons and crash-test dummies didn't convince everyone. Many people still believe that aliens have visited Earth. "The only dummies in the whole thing would be us if we believed a word of this," said UFO researcher Dennis Balthaser.

Balthaser and other believers are certain that aliens crashed near Roswell in 1947. Dozens of books argue that the U.S. military knows what happened and has covered it up for decades. If that is true, it is one of the greatest conspiracies in modern history.

## Seeing Is Believing

But if what the military said is true, why did so many people claim to have seen evidence of aliens at Roswell? Were they looking for attention? Did they just want to believe in alien contact?

Or did aliens really crash in the New Mexico desert?

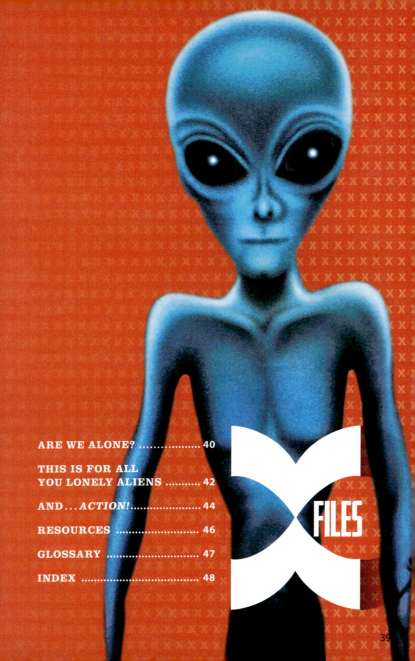

| ARE WE ALONE? | 40 |
| THIS IS FOR ALL YOU LONELY ALIENS | 42 |
| AND...*ACTION!* | 44 |
| RESOURCES | 46 |
| GLOSSARY | 47 |
| INDEX | 48 |

X FILES

# Are We Alone?

**This astronomer keeps his eyes open for evidence of life in outer space.**

**SETH SHOSTAK** is an astronomer at the SETI Institute (SETI stands for Search for Extraterrestrial Intelligence).

**How did you get interested in SETI?**
**SHOSTAK:** I've liked astronomy since I was eight. I built a telescope when I was ten. In middle school, I became interested in aliens. Then I studied physics in college. I switched to astronomy in graduate school because it seemed more romantic. I was studying galaxies with radio telescopes. It dawned on me that the telescopes could be used to see whether there really are aliens.

**The radio telescope scans for radio waves. Do you ever look through a regular telescope?**
**SHOSTAK:** Only amateur astronomers look through [light] telescopes anymore. Your eyes are great for some things but not for seeing faint objects. And you don't even have to be at the radio telescope to check for signals. The computer does that and sends the data to your desktop computer.

**IN DEPTH**

### Have you ever thought you had received a signal from aliens?

**SHOSTAK:** One time we accidentally picked up a signal from a satellite. It looked like it might be an [alien], but our equipment just wasn't working. We did find out what would happen if we ever do get an alien signal. The word leaked out, and we started getting calls from reporters right away.

### How has SETI research changed during your career?

**SHOSTAK:** The equipment is not just millions, not just billions, not just trillions, but hundreds of trillions times faster and more sensitive. We also know more than we did in 1960 when the first SETI experiment was planned. We thought there *might* be planets around other stars, but now we *know* there are. That makes us smarter about where to point our telescopes.

### Do you believe it's possible there are other forms of life in the universe?

**SHOSTAK:** [Life might exist on] many billions of worlds... Life may be plentiful beyond what is easy to imagine.

**HUGE RADIO TELESCOPES** like these at the Very Large Array observatory in New Mexico are used to detect data from objects in outer space.

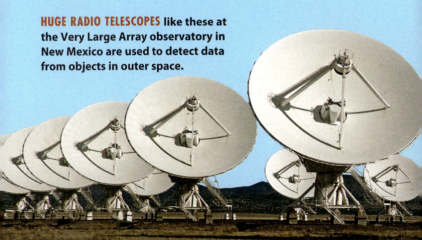

# This Is for All You Lonely Aliens

**Here's how some scientists tried to send messages to space aliens.**

In 1977, NASA launched *Voyager 1* and *2*. These spacecraft carry identical 12-inch, gold-plated phonograph records. The sounds and images on the records are meant to show the "diversity of life and culture on Earth" to alien beings.

The images include male and female bodies, snowflakes, trees, dolphins, and a supermarket. Sounds include wind, thunder, bird and whale calls, music from various cultures, and greetings in 55 languages.

Aliens won't receive this greeting any time soon. Since leaving our solar system, the spacecraft have been drifting through empty space. They won't approach another star for at least 40,000 years.

This shows the needle positioned to play the record from the beginning. The lines around the disc are meant to explain how fast to spin the record.

## IN DEPTH

These drawings show how to convert the coded signals on the record into pictures.

The cover is coated with uranium-238 (U-238). Uranium decays at a steady rate. This makes it a kind of radioactive clock. By analyzing the amount of U-238 left, a smart alien could figure out how long the spacecraft has been traveling from Earth.

This is the side of the record that plays sounds.

This is a copy of the first picture on the record. It is meant to show the aliens that they've decoded the record correctly.

This is a map that shows the location of our solar system.

This is a side view of the record and needle. The lines represent numbers that tell how long it takes to play one side.

# And... Action!

## These space aliens landed in the movies.

One of the first movies ever made featured aliens. Titled *A Trip to the Moon*, it was made in 1902. Since then, many popular movies have been made about aliens or space travel. These films show how we imagine what extraterrestrials might look like (pretty weird) and how they might behave (badly, for the most part).

## Monstrous...

The big-headed beings in *Invasion of the Saucer-Men* (right, 1957) and *Mars Attacks!* (far right, 1996) are typical of how Hollywood has portrayed aliens.

The aliens in *Earth vs. the Flying Saucers* (left, 1956) destroy most of Washington, D.C., before they are defeated.

## ...or

**IN DEPTH**

## or Movie Stars?

But not all movie aliens have huge heads. Some, like those in *The Man from Planet X* (right, 1951) and *The Brother From Another Planet* (far right, 1985), look a lot like humans.

## Nasty Invaders . . .

The attackers in *Strange Invaders* (left, 1983) take over the bodies of people in a small midwestern town.

In *War of the Worlds* (left, 2005), aliens in giant machines try to wipe out humankind.

## Friendly Beings?

In *Close Encounters of the Third Kind* (left, 1977), a giant UFO lands on Earth. But the aliens on board have come to make friends with humans, not to destroy them.

In *E.T.* (left, 1982), a cute alien is stranded on Earth. The little guy doesn't want to hurt anyone—he just wants to go home.

# RESOURCES

**Here's a selection of books and websites for more information about UFOs.**

## What to Read Next

### NONFICTION

Firestone, Mary. *SETI Scientist* (Weird Careers in Science). Broomall, PA: Chelsea House, 2005.

Grace, N. B. *UFOs: What Scientists Say May Shock You!* New York: Franklin Watts, 2008.

Jackson, Ellen. *Looking for Life in the Universe: The Search for Extraterrestrial Intelligence.* New York: Houghton Mifflin, 2005.

Krull, Kathleen. *What Really Happened in Roswell? Just the Facts (Plus the Rumors) About UFOs and Aliens.* New York: HarperCollins, 2003.

Mason, Paul. *Investigating UFOs* (Forensic Files). Chicago: Heinemann, 2004.

Roleff, Tamara L. *Alien Abductions* (Fact or Fiction?). Chicago: Greenhaven Press, 2003.

Skurzynski, Gloria. *Are We Alone? Scientists Search for Life in Space.* Washington, DC: National Geographic Children's Books, 2004.

### FICTION

Anaya, Rudolfo. *ChupaCabra and the Roswell UFO.* Albuquerque, NM: University of New Mexico Press, 2008.

Coville, Bruce, ed. *Bruce Coville's UFOs.* New York: Avon Books, 2000.

Rex, Adam. *The True Meaning of Smekday.* New York: Hyperion Books for Children, 2007.

Teitelbaum, Michael. *The Scary States of America.* New York: Delacorte Press, 2007.

## Websites

### J. Allen Hynek Center for UFO Studies (CUFOS)
**www.cufos.org/index.html**
This group of international scientists, investigators, professors, and volunteers is dedicated to the examination and analysis of UFO information.

### National UFO Reporting Center
**www.ufocenter.com**
At this site, users can report UFO sightings or read about UFO history and interesting recent sightings.

# GLOSSARY

**abducted** (ub-DUKT-ed) *adjective* taken away by force; kidnapped

**astronomer** (uh-STRON-uh-mur) *noun* a scientist who studies the universe by observing planets, stars, and galaxies

**autopsy** (AW-top-see) *noun* a surgical examination of a dead body

**conspiracy** (kun-SPEER-uh-see) *noun* a secret plot or scheme

**debris** (deh-BREE) *noun* scattered pieces of something that has been destroyed

**evidence** (EV-uh-duhnss) *noun* information that helps establish the truth about something

**extraterrestrial** (EK-struh-tur-ess-tree-ul) *noun* a being that comes from outer space

**high-altitude** (HYE-AL-tih-tood) *adjective* very high above the ground

**hoax** (HOHX) *noun* an elaborate trick

**implanted** (IM-plant-ed) *adjective* inserted into the tissue of a human or other animal

**investigate** (in-VESS-tuh-gate) *verb* to find out as much as possible about something

**laser** (LAY-zur) *noun* a very narrow, powerful beam of light

**nuclear weapon** (NOO-klee-ur WEP-uhn) *noun* a weapon that uses the power created by splitting atoms

**radioactive** (ray-dee-oh-AK-tiv) *adjective* made up of atoms whose nuclei break down, giving off harmful energy

**satellite** (SAT-uh-lyte) *noun* a spacecraft that orbits Earth or other bodies in space. Some satellites transmit TV signals and others monitor activity on Earth.

**skeptic** (SKEP-tik) *noun* someone who doubts or questions ideas or beliefs

**tabloid** (TAB-loyd) *noun* a newspaper dominated by headlines, photographs, and sensational stories

**theory** (THIHR-ee) *noun* an idea based on some facts or evidence but not proved

**weather balloon** (WETH-ur buh-LOON) *noun* a balloon that is sent into the atmosphere to gather information about the weather

# INDEX

abductions, 15, 21, *21*
*Alien Autopsy: Fact or Fiction?* television show, 34–35, *34*
aliens, 14, 15, 21, *21*, *22*, 23–27, *24*, *26–27*, 31, 32, 34–35, *34*, 37, 38, 40–41, 42–43, 44–45, *44–45*
astronomers, 29, *29*, 40–41, *40*
autopsies, 26, *26–27*, 31, 34–35, *34*

ball lightning, 29, *29*
balloons, 19, 28, *30*, 32, *33*, 37
Balthaser, Dennis, 37
Barnett, Grady L., 23–24
Belleville, Wisconsin, 34–35, *34*
books, 37–38
Brazel, W. W. "Mac," 11–12, 13, 17, 24, 32

Carter, Jimmy, 15
Clark, Chuck, 29, *29*
close encounters, 21, *21*
Corso, Philip J., 27
crash site, 11–12, 20, 23–24, *24*, *36*
crash-test dummies, 32, *33*, 37

debris, 11–12, *12*, 13, 17, *18*, 19, 20, *20*, 21, *21*, 24, 26–27, 30, 32

Eighth Army Air Force, 19
eyewitnesses, 15, 21, 23–25, 28, 29, 35, 38

"Flying Cigar," 34–35, *34*

Hangar, *18*, 25, 26–27
Hoagland, Hudson, 15
hoaxes, 29, *29*
Humphreys, John, 35

Illinois Air Traffic Control, 35
implants, 15, *15*
International UFO Museum and Research Center, *26–27*

Kaufman, Frank, 24

landing sites, 15
Lubbock, Texas, 34–35, *34*

Marcel, Jesse, 17, 19, 20, *20*, 23
military. *See* U.S. Air Force; U.S. Army.
movies, 44–45, *44–45*

NASA, 42
*National Enquirer* newspaper, 20
newspaper reports, 12–13, 19–20

phonograph record, 42–43, *42–43*
photographs, 15, *15*
pilots, 13, 25
Project Blue Book, 28–29
Project Mogul, 31, 32

radio telescopes, 40, *41*
researchers, 21, 23, 25
Roswell Army Air Field, 13, 17, 19, 20, 24, 25, 32
Roswell, New Mexico, 11, 12, *16*, 23, 31, 35, 37–38, *37*

SETI (Search for Extraterrestrial Intelligence), 40–41, *41*
Shostak, Seth, 40–41, *40*
skeptics, 14, 15, 21
spy planes, 28

technology, 27, 32, 40, 41, *41*

uranium, 42–43
U.S. Air Force, 19, 25, 26–27, 28, *30*, 31, 32, *33*, 37
U.S. Army, 13, 17, *18*, 19, 20, 24, *24*, 25, 25, 27, 32

*Voyager* spacecraft, 42

weather, 29, *29*
wreckage. *See* debris.
Wright-Patterson Air Force Base, 25, 26–27

## METRIC CONVERSIONS

**Feet to meters:** 1 ft is about 0.3 m
**Miles to kilometers:** 1 mi is about 1.6 km
**Pounds to kilograms:** 1 lb is about 0.45 kg
**Ounces to grams:** 1 oz is about 28 g